CHEETAHS

by Jaclyn Jaycox

PEBBLE
a capstone imprint

Pebble Explore is published by Pebble, an imprint of Capstone.
1710 Roe Crest Drive
North Mankato, Minnesota 56003
www.capstonepub.com

Library of Congress Cataloging-in-Publication data is available on the Library of Congress website.
ISBN 978-1-9771-2314-5 (library binding)
ISBN 978-1-9771-2648-1 (paperback)
ISBN 978-1-9771-2322-0 (eBook PDF)

Summary: Text describes cheetahs, including where they live, their bodies, what they do, and dangers to cheetahs.

Image Credits
Capstone Press, 6; Newscom: Suzi Eszterhas/Minden Pictures, 22; Shutterstock: AfricaWildlife, 1, ben landy, 11, Bildagentur Zoonar GmbH, Cover, Fiona Ayerst, 28, GUDKOV ANDREY, 21, 24, JonathanC Photography, 5, knelson20, 18, Mostafa A. Elbrolosy, 25, Olga Kashubin, 7, Robart Mwaiteleke, 13, rokopix, 8, Ryan M. Bolton, 16, Shahin Olakara, 17, Stuart G Porter, 10, Tony Campbell, 26, Victor Lapaev, 15

Editorial Credits
Editor: Mandy Robbins; Designer: Dina Her; Media Researcher: Morgan Walters; Production Specialist: Tori Abraham

All internet sites appearing in back matter were available and accurate when this book was sent to press.

Printed in the United States of America.
PA117

Table of Contents

Words in **bold** are in the glossary.

Amazing Cheetahs

What can run three times faster than a human? Do you need a hint? It has four legs and spots. If you guessed a cheetah, you're right! It is the fastest animal on land.

Cheetahs are in the cat family. They are a type of **mammal**. Mammals can breathe air. They have hair or fur. They give birth to live young.

Where in the World

Cheetahs are found in Africa. A small number of them also live in Iran. They are found in warm **habitats**. They live in deserts and grasslands. They also live in woodlands and **savannas**.

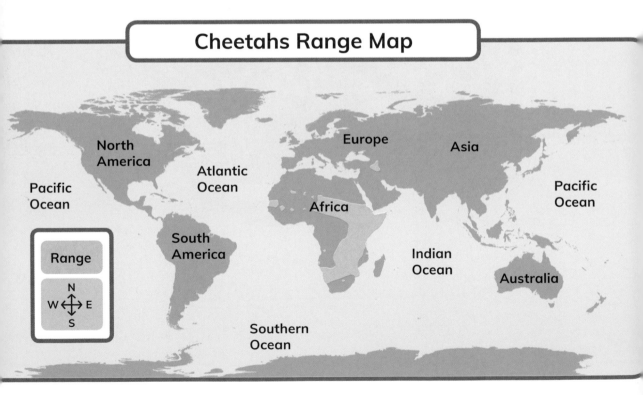

Cheetahs Range Map

North America

Europe

Asia

Atlantic Ocean

Pacific Ocean

Pacific Ocean

Africa

South America

Indian Ocean

Australia

Range

N
W E
S

Southern Ocean

Cheetahs spend their time in wide-open areas. They sleep under trees. The trees give them shelter and shade. They may also rest in tall grass.

Cheetah Bodies

Cheetahs are known for their spots. They have about 2,000 black spots on their fur. They also have black rings around their tails.

Each cheetah has a different **pattern** of spots and rings. The markings help the big cats blend into their surroundings. When they hunt, they can sneak up on **prey**. They can also hide from animals that hunt them.

Cheetahs have tan or yellow fur. They have white throats and bellies. Black lines run from their eyes to their mouths.

Cheetahs can be up to 30 inches
(76 centimeters) tall. They can grow
56 inches (142 cm) long. Adults weigh
up to 140 pounds (64 kilograms).
Males are a little bigger than females.

Cheetahs have small heads. They have brown eyes. They have great eyesight during the day. They can see up to 3 miles (5 kilometers) away. But they cannot see well at night.

Cheetahs are great runners. They have long, skinny bodies. They have long legs too. Their big lungs take in a lot of air. This helps them breathe while running. Cheetahs can run up to 70 miles (113 km) per hour.

Cheetahs have special paw pads. The pads help them grip the ground when running. It takes cheetahs just three seconds to reach speeds of 60 miles (97 km) per hour!

On the Menu

It's early morning. A cheetah sits on top of a hill. It looks out over the grass. It spots an **antelope**. The cheetah slowly sneaks toward it. Suddenly, it runs after its prey. Zoom! The cheetah catches its meal in seconds.

Cheetahs are meat eaters. They eat antelope and **warthogs**. They eat birds and rabbits too.

Cheetahs hunt in the morning or afternoon. They can see better then. Other big cats hunt at night. Cheetahs stay away from them.

A cheetah has small teeth and jaws. It catches its prey by tripping it. Then it bites the animal's throat.

Cheetahs don't always catch
their prey. They get tired quickly.
They can only run at high speeds
for a short time.

Cheetahs sometimes carry prey to a hiding spot. They try to eat fast. Bigger cats may come to take their food. Cheetahs won't fight them. They run away.

Cheetahs eat about 6 pounds (3 kg) of food a day. They drink very little water. It can be hard to find water where they live. They only need one drink every three or four days.

Life of a Cheetah

Male cheetahs live in groups. Adult females live alone. Males and females only come together to **mate**. Cheetahs mate at all times of the year.

Females have up to eight babies. Baby cheetahs are called cubs. They are about 12 inches (30 cm) long. They weigh about 12 ounces (340 grams). Cubs are born with all their spots. They have long gray fur down their backs. It helps them blend in to the tall grass.

Females raise cubs on their own. Cubs drink milk from their mother. They can walk after just a few weeks. A mother moves her cubs to a new place almost every day. That way **predators** have a harder time finding them.

Sometimes a mother and her cubs get too far apart. They make a chirping sound to find each other.

Cubs start to eat meat at six weeks
old. At six months old, their mother
teaches them to hunt. Cubs also learn
to hunt by playing together. They
sneak up and jump on each other.

At 15 months, cheetahs are fully grown. Their mother will leave them at about 18 months. The cubs stay together for six more months. Then females will go off on their own. The males stay together for life. Cheetahs usually live between 10 and 12 years.

Dangers to Cheetahs

Adult cheetahs are rarely killed by predators. But most cubs don't survive. Lions attack cubs. Leopards and hyenas do too. Only about one in 10 cubs lives longer than three months.

Humans are a threat to cheetahs. People use more and more land for farming. Cheetahs are losing their homes. So is their prey. Soon, cheetahs may not have enough to eat. People also hunt cheetahs for their fur.

The number of cheetahs is going down. There may be fewer than 8,000 left. But people are working to help them. They are learning more about cheetahs. They are protecting the land where they live.

Fast Facts

Name: cheetah

Habitat: deserts, grasslands, savannas, woodlands

Where in the World : Africa and Iran

Food: antelope, warthogs, birds, rabbits

Predators: lions, leopards, hyenas

Life span: 10 to 12 years

Glossary

antelope (AN-tuh-lohp)—an animal that looks like a large deer and runs very fast

habitat (HAB-uh-tat)—the natural place and conditions in which an animal or plant lives

mammal (MAM-uhl)—a warm–blooded animal that breathes air; mammals have hair or fur; female mammals feed milk to their young

mate (MATE)—to join together to produce young

pattern (PAT-urn)—a repeating arrangement of colors and shapes

predator (PRED-uh-tur)—an animal that hunts other animals for food

prey (PRAY)—an animal hunted by another animal for food

savanna (suh-VAN-uh)—a flat, grassy area of land with few or no trees

warthog (WORT-hog)—a wild African pig with large tusks

Read More

Amstutz, Lisa J. *A Day in the Life of a Cheetah: A 4D Book*. North Mankato, MN: an imprint of Pebble, 2019.

Klukow, Mary Ellen. *Cheetahs*. Mankato, MN: Amicus, 2020.

Unwin, Cynthia. *Cheetahs*. New York: Children's Press, an imprint of Scholastic, Inc., 2019.

Internet Sites

African Cheetah
kids.sandiegozoo.org/animals/african-cheetah

Cheetah Conservation Fund Kids
cheetah.org/kids/cheetah-facts/

Cheetahs
kids.nationalgeographic.com/animals/mammals/cheetah/

Index